I0200399

A Breath of *Melodies*

Inspiring Souls

Denise P. Ford

A Breath of *Melodies*

Revision, September 2023

Copyright © 2006 by Denise P. Ford

All rights reserved. No part of this book may be reproduced or transmitted in any form or by any means without written permission of the author.

The content of this book is based on actual accounts; and the words of inspiration were given by divine revelation through the Holy Spirit.

Scriptures noted NKJV are taken from the New King James Version®.

Copyright© 1982 by Thomas Nelson, Inc. Used by permission. All rights reserved.

ISBN 978-0-9830162-0-5

Visit www.amazon.com to order additional copies.

Dedication

I dedicate this work in loving memory to my grandparents, the late Bishop Ceasar A. Ford and Betty B. Ford. You were true farmers and fishers of men. Part of who you were lives on inside of me, your legacy of hard work and spirit of sowing. The harvest will be plentiful as the seeds fall on good ground. Thank you to my friend and husband, Thomas E. Walker for believing in me.

Acknowledgments

God is the source to everything that has life. First and foremost, I honor and praise Him, for giving me the gift of words to share. I have accepted my assignment to serve God. All of my work is a kingdom effort: the kingdom of all God's people working together to exhibit love for one another.

Thank you to my family, I love you.

Contents

Introduction

The struggles of life can sometimes seem devastating, because it can cause the soul to commit suicide, lie, steal, kill, and perform the regrettable. I'm here to share some good news of hope. If you can start your day out by reading a positive word sent from above, you will activate the spirit realm. The Lord has allowed His people to gain hope, love, and prosperity through His written word. If you believe in the Holy Bible, you will find "Naima's Inspirational Melodies," a collection of uniquely spiritual poems, to minister to your soul.

Words are powerful. You can produce life and death by the words you speak. If you feed your mind with good reading and loving thoughts, it will create the kind of life that you desire. As you live, you will walk right into that kind of life. The melodies of God's heart will lead your soul to the fountain of grace where there's healing, deliverance, restoration, and peace that flows like the rushing rivers. As your soul prospers in the intangible gifts that are given from above, your thinking will change. You can't buy the intangible gifts with money; such good gifts are blessings that await your prayers as God answers your needs.

Everything that He creates was given a purpose, to fulfill a plan that only He designed for His will. As we learn through the scriptures, it is His will that we seek Him first and obey His command. Through surrendering, we must first believe in His word of truth and search through it, seeking all things that He has ordained and placed in our paths to draw us closer to the abundance of His prosperity.

By grace and mercy, you don't have to do anything but believe and make that choice today to trust God in all things. Whatever you need or desire, it is written that you must ask, seek and knock in order to reap from His storehouse. I am blessed to be used as a vessel that the Lord has predestined to introduce to the world the spiritual inspirations of "Reflections of Grace Outreach Ministries." Faith, love, health, healing, prosperity, and an abundance of wealth can be supported through sowing the word of God into the lives of people who are in transition to a breakthrough for better living.

Somehow we take part in forming the life that we want by speaking things into existence and journaling our thoughts and the things that we have experienced. Please allow your heart to dream. I caution you to speak positive things into the universe and watch how things manifest.

As you read through the memories of my journey and the melodies of God's heart, I believe that you will be inspired to leave the past, live in the present, and walk into the future.

Reflections of God's Grace

The Past

As I look back over my troubled life, if it had not been for the bad things that happened to me, I would have never been able to see the power of God. I lived in the shadows of my ancestor's faith and built my beliefs on the many stories that were passed down to me.

Since learning that I survived what some people were unfortunately unable to endure, I credit that to how I was raised in the church at an early age. It prepared me to know whom to call when I fell into various trials and troubles in the name of Jesus. That was more important to my grandparents, who finished raising me.

My faith was developed through the storms and mountains that I had to climb. I had no sense of direction and was clueless about many things, until I had to endure them. As the old saying goes, charity starts at home. It is crucial to have someone teach you at an early age about life, too. The foundation of love was never taught to me by my parents. Therefore, I looked for it and accepted whatever scraps that appeared to be love.

On many occasions, I opened the doors to allowing the hurt that I experienced from others. But over the years, the anger that I carried in my heart was restored by the love of Christ. The principles of love and forgiveness will teach you many things about yourself and others. I can wear a smile on my face because I've learned what it means to let go of negative baggage; it holds you back. I am thankful to be a survivor and knowing that the pain from my past does not determine my outcome.

A New Day, the Present

Time does fly, and trouble doesn't last always. It's kind of funny as I sit and ponder about how I perceive life. Many prayers have been answered, and I've lived to tell it. The faces that I was familiar with are no longer around. I've traveled many paths and walked in circles to find myself back at the beginning again. I didn't know it, but the road does get narrow. It can take days, years, and decades to find the right road.

Today my life is different; I have been given a second chance. There's so much to do now that I have focus and a purpose. As I pray daily, I don't worry anymore about the future. I've matured spiritually in many aspects, and I understand a majority of the lessons. The wisdom and understanding that I've prayed for has blossomed. I'm drawn to and I appreciate sitting under great wisdom when it presents itself.

I have been blessed to be remarried and united with a God fearing man. Since our journeys have joined together, we are building a legacy of faith and hope through "Reflections of Grace Outreach Ministries." I never thought that my life could be used in such a way that would bring my creator the glory. God has a way of showing you things when you are mature enough to receive them. I am in tune and listening to His direction for my life. My mind is renewed, and that's because I'm spending time getting to know Him. I know that my strength comes from the Lord. A true change starts within the heart. Only God can take a remnant of something that was rejected and broken and design a fine piece of art. Besides, He's the creator and it's entirely up to Him in the first place to shape and mold me.

He knows the reason why He created my life. I'm standing on the foundation of His word. There's no looking to the left or the right. It's evident that His way is the right path. On the days when life seems hard, I can find something to smile about because in all of this He causes me to triumph over my enemies. Therefore, I will obey the call on my life and let my light so shine, while it's day. There's much work to do in the vineyard.

The Future

Truly no one knows what the future holds, but with prayer and focus, dreams can come true. Since knowing that my life was transitioned to a spiritual calling, I've been laboring for God. When I meditate about the future, I am vigilant about staying on the path to fulfilling my life's purpose.

As my mind drifted back and forth through time, what can I say most about life? I am at peace with myself. My character has been shaped into a better human being. I don't have to have everything I desire; I no longer have to be a part of what's happening in the social scene, to know what's going on in other folk's lives to measure mine, or to compare myself to others.

I've been busy over the past six years, writing and searching for the next step that God has ordained for my life. It can be a full-time job, waiting and listening to Him for signs and wonders. The course that's been charted for me has been full of adventure and of course anxiety of the unknown. The greatest part about the journey? I realized a way has already been made for me to succeed.

I haven't prepared a dream list, because the road I'm traveling has been colorful. The sun is bright, the skies are blue, and when it rains, I take things slow while I find a place to rest. The people who have crossed my path have shown me some form of kindness, favor, and mercy. I trust that it is a part of the plan. I am so thankful, because things are in motion.

As I look to the future, I am reminded of how eagles fly. They have the ability to soar high, keen eye sight, and the determination to balance the power that is given to them. I attribute the inspiration that I have been given to God as a gift enabling me to be used as an instrument for the enlightenment and the good of others.

Since surrendering my heart to God, I have decided to rest from my cares and concerns. I trust that God has what my life was created for all figured out. But through every great mission, there will be testing, a process of building, planting, sowing, and reaping. Therefore, I will keep treading and laboring until the mission is won.

CHAPTER 1

Absolutely

The years are passing, and I've discovered something that's been consistent: God's love. I wouldn't trade places to be anyone else, because He's shown me a better way to live through His love.

People have taught me many things about myself that I never knew existed, until I was at my wit's end. I opened many doors to following people down paths that only caused me disappointments, pain, and hurt. For many years, I was searching for love and happiness, but always falling short.

When I finally stop crying over the mistakes that I had made and feeling sorry for myself, that's when I received my miracle. I was blessed by God when He opened my eyes to turn to Him. I've taken my eyes off of depending on others and have prioritized some things differently in my life by putting God first. Since spending time alone in prayer, it has become my resting place.

I wasn't the smartest or prettiest, and I've always settled for less. I've missed the mark more than I can recount. Yes, I'm thankful for my weaknesses, shortcomings, and inadequacies, because I can boast about just how good God is. I lift my hands, because my strength, abilities, and talent can't replace His infinite wisdom. There's no other way to put it—He is the source, my source, "absolutely."

The passion is burning inside my heart to give Him more. I am only an instrument waiting to obey what He commands. There's laughter and joy behind the music, when I sit to ponder the melodies.

Although I've been through many storms, I am reminded of something my aunt says about me, "You are a tree planted." I may bend or lean when the winds blow, but my roots are deep. One day my tree will grow tall and stand strong when the stormy winds blow.

I am passionately lost inside of my emotions about why God loves me. I used to wonder what He thinks about me, but since my blessings are infinite I have concluded that it's true love. Therefore, He's in control and I'm absolutely His.

Joy Bells

When my heart is filled with tears
I will hold to the scriptures
As life bears its sorrow
There's a longing in my soul
As I pray for peace and contentment
My mourning will turn to dancing
While quieting my spirit to listen
My heart starts racing
While closing my eyes
Images of angels appear
Holding bright lights
Echoing sweet sounds of praise
While spreading their wings
Releasing joy and comfort
As my tears rain from grace

Sweet Grace

My lips are full of praise
Words of peace and joy I sing
Heaven I adore Your glory
As the angels spread their wings
A whisper of Your presence fills the air
Holiness flows from Your feet
Sweet Jesus, sweet Jesus
You are that secret place
While my soul sings
Let Your power and Spirit embrace
Rain and pour Your sweet mercy
I am delighted
As I stand in the midst of paradise
I'll keep praising and singing my all
You are holier than any miracle
For my spirit is mesmerized
Sweet love, sweet love unconditional
Oh my soul says yes, I'll serenade

My Lord
God, You are beautiful
Sweeter than the air
Brighter than any glory
As I breathe Your grace
My soul sings for mercy
As it rains from the throne
Your aura knows my heart
As it beats passionately and intimately
While resting inside Your care
As the earth bears its fruit
My praise shall witness
The light that shines
A majesty that governs eternity
Through the wind and rain
Your word is everlasting

Exalt His Love
As I breathe through my nostrils
I will be mindful to say thank You
Liberty, grace, and mercy
I will never be able to say it enough
For time is not on my side as I live
Each sunrise and sunset
I will witness Your love to others
By learning to smile when I am sad
I will laugh when the tears fall
For I know that You are there
No tear is hidden from You
Every sunrise obeys Your command
When I exalt You through my writings
I pray that others receive Your word
Because there's nothing more everlasting

Excellent

Marvelous wonderful to my soul
There is peace and joy when I sing
Hallelujah to the name of Jesus
A comforter through all seasons
As bright as the sun shines
Praise belong to the Spirit of truth
When You breathe life into my being
I speak Your name
A power that moves heaven and earth
Creator of lights to whom I honor
Oh excellence the mark of grace
The blood that covers all sins
When I call on the name of Jesus
A love that is proven
His glory exudes the light of the world

Breathtaking

As my soul breathes
I am passionately humbled
My heart is fluttering
I am at a loss for words
As the music plays
While my heart listens
I am alive and my spirit is free
How amazing
A love that captures the heart
As it spreads around the throne
Miracles of glory
My soul is filled
I will cherish and fathom
While I live my life praying
Absolutely breathtaking

CHAPTER 2

A Bouquet of Blessings

As I anticipate spring each year, my soul is filled with joy. There's something special about this time of year. The air is fresh, the smell of cut grass, flowers are in bloom. I'm thankful for having an open mind. My soul is calm; I have so many things to be thankful for as I ponder my health, family, and purpose.

There were times in my life when I felt surprised after receiving a bouquet of flowers. I love roses, tulips, orchids, and azaleas among others. Women are so fascinated by surrounding themselves with the aura and beauty that flowers bring. We cherish the memories, especially when it's from someone whom we love or are in love with. Some of my greatest memories are still vivid in my heart.

My life has been touched by the kindness and thoughtfulness of others that took the next step in showing me that they cared. I supposed that I may have planted a seed of kindness in return, because I was reaping blessings. Although I have had some happy times, I've had plenty of sick days, sad ones, too, and many storms. I am free to celebrate how I am much stronger because of it.

The old adage is true: "Give me my flowers while I live." If you love someone, now is the time to give them your best. Show your support; tell them how much they mean to you. It doesn't have to be in the form of a tangible gift.

Once I broke down in tears because I was caught by surprise. My niece was visiting me, and she visited my church during her stay. She's very shy, and when she was asked by my pastor if she had any words she'd like to say, everyone was quiet. As she spoke about being blessed, alive, and giving her praise to God, she looked at me and begin to speak such warm, heartfelt words about me. She started crying as she continued to speak. My eyes became full of tears, and my heart started pounding fast. My goodness, I wasn't prepared for it. My mascara started smearing, and it took me some time to calm down. I reached out to give her a hug while holding her tightly; my pastor told her not to apologize for crying and prolonging the time, but to give me my flowers while I live.

That experience allowed me to witness how many years it could take to sow good seeds into the lives of others before you start to reap in yours. God has your days marked on His calendar when it's your time to receive your bouquet. I count my blessings, because my sad days weren't too far away.

As you stop to think about your life, always remember that God has given you a bouquet of blessings by allowing you to still be here and have the activity of your being. Don't complain about what others won't do for you, but find ways to bless someone who doesn't have it as good as you. It will spring forth blessings in your own life when you least expect it. There's no greater gift when you have deposited love, kindness, and blessed words into someone else's heart.

The Weed or the Flower

As life unfolds your dream
Pray for the impossible
For blessings are waiting
As you labor you are sowing
Keep speaking it into existence
While the answers take form
Sometimes doubt will come
You must remain true
Success will come if you continue
Be not dismayed if you see some weeds
A new season will arrive
If you trust in the divine law
For a flower will bloom
There will be rain, testing, and fruit
For God is working to fulfill His mysteries

Rainbows

Lord, I know that You love me
You send rainbows after the storm
When I see the many colors from above
I smile because I know You are watching
My eyes can see Your beauty inside and out
I appreciate all that You've done in my life
I fear You and want more of Your love
You've given me sight to rejoice
Every color that You reveal
I am not alone when rainbows stop by
No matter how many storms come
My soul can rest in peace and depend on Your love

Butterfly Angels
While I live to see God's love
May He richly bless my soul
In the valley of the lilies I will pray
When signs and wonders come
Butterflies gather to dance
While feeling the warmth of the sun
As my heart flutters to and fro
It's truly amazing to feel such splendor
Upon the path to eternity
When love is present I will breathe
As the flowers bloom forth
My soul shall sing
How gracious and sweet
To every blessing that appears
Rays of living colors
Etched from wing to wing
Touching every soul that lives
While imparting God's love

Fresh Flowers
As my soul prospers
I will rise with a smile
For my soul knows it well
The angels are rejoicing
As I face the doors to prosperity
It's truly amazing and beautiful
While I continue to sow seeds
I can see the buds in bloom
May God's glory reign forever
Whispers of love and joy
As I breathe and sing His praises
To the angels as they bless
My heart will always be thankful
As I live to rejoice and dance
While I fathom the day
My breakthrough is near
Oh, how lovely and sweet it is
To behold what is mine

Smell the Flowers

I see the beauty of Your heart, Lord
I feel excited when I am loved
Nothing else matters
Everything that You create has purpose
And while I live to fulfill my destiny
I will learn to cherish my flowers
I understand that they are made special
I will learn to remember their scent
When I touch their lips I feel how Your heart feels
When I am loved
Thank You for blessing my life

365 Days

Each day of the year pray to Me
I have given you a calendar
There's no greater planner than Mine
I have set aside to hear your thoughts
I'm giving you grace and mercy
If you schedule Me in I'll show you
Seasons come to remind you
Don't take for granted another 365 days
I'm willing to give you eternal life
If you believe and take heed
I'll put your blessings on My calendar
You will receive everyone on time

CHAPTER 3

Summer Skies

When blue skies hang low, I believe I can touch the sky. There are so many reasons I could think of why I feel so blessed, but the two that I give thanks to the most are having life and my sight to see, because without it, a painting worth a million dollars would be meaningless. As I make plans each day to embrace the universe, I'm elated. My heart is full of wonder and compassion, because I'm no longer chasing material things to complete me.

I've learned to put some things into perspective; I've found freedom in the walks that I spend alone. The things that I use to worry about seem to lessen. The bills will always be there; somebody is going to leave me for some reason or another, and dislike me. I am aging gracefully, and the music will fade. But what seems to hold true is that time is not on my side, and I've learned to grasp what I have been given and that is to see life clearly.

There were times when I thought I had to have what I wanted. But after I worked hard and borrowed on credit to get some of the things I yearned for, I realized that it wasn't the thing that I needed or wanted. My closets were filled and cluttered with clothing, shoes, and stuff. Sometimes, I felt cheated and saddened after checking my bank account and realizing that I didn't have enough funds to make ends meet or enough to get to the next pay day without borrowing or doing without.

One day I finally got off the merry-go-round and decided to give away some of my earthly things that caused me to feel so empty and broke. It made the difference, because now I have a panoramic view. The portrait of my life paints a soft scene; it's a delicate blend of nature and colors that radiate the things, places, and people who have added joy to my life.

There's balance in my life and my soul sings, because it's so liberating. There's another world that exists outside of life's demands, and stresses; it evolves through seasons. The season that I love most is the summer; it's my favorite time of year. When the music stops playing, the seasons will continue to change no matter who's listening.

As I walk outside to greet the summer skies, I am smiling. I'm delighted to continue the journey, because I've learned that seasons come to prepare me while I go through life's transitions. Therefore, I will let go of yesterday, so I can live in the present. While it's still summer, I am reminded of my blessings as I bask and play in the sunlight.

Down on my Knees

I'm thankful for Your love
As I climb out of bed through mercy and grace
I'm on my knees with my praise
Father, I could have been dead in my sleep
But through the blood my body is able
I'm alive and I can do all things through Christ
I don't deserve Your goodness
If I can please You, Lord, what must I do?
When You rain Your blessings upon my soul
I have my health and I'm in my right mind
No matter what the day may bring
I know You woke me up this morning to pray
Give me, dear Lord, the right words
Allow my spirit to receive
As I lift my hands toward heaven

Highest of High

His glory brightens the sky
The sun and the moon obeys
While nature fulfills its purpose
There are two spheres that exist
Heaven and earth are in His hands
As He breathes within the universe
Doves, butterflies, and lilies
Awe to capture such beauty
As the wind blows upon the sea
What a passion to honor
The sounds of drums beating
Resounding through the universe
Jesus, Your name our hearts rejoice
We seek Your kingdom as Your will be done
Together we sing in harmony

Traveling Grace

While traveling through life
Lord, watch over my soul
I realize my life is not my own
I'm only human, but my fears are real
I speak life and protection to my mind
I have work to do and it's not complete
You've revealed my purpose
Please allow my life to bring You glory
I want to fulfill my assignment
I know that You are in control over all situations
I thank You for sparing my life
I pray this prayer in Jesus' name

Guide My Soul

When the day has come to an end
My soul shall ponder
If today should be my last
I have stumbled and strayed
As I face the moment
I pray to You, dear Lord
The race is not given to the swift
My heart is cheering
I will not give up when I am weak
As I strive to move forward
I will walk in the light
For Your grace and mercy sustains me

Presence of Glory

When I look towards heaven
My soul says yes to You, dear Lord
As I feel the warmth of the sun
I am truly amazed to see Your art
Your beauty radiates in all things
I've even learned to walk in the rain
My heart is beating so rapidly
While I witness another day
The air is sweet and flowers are in bloom
The wind blows and whispers
I pray to remain humble
As nature rejoices in the midst

Ribbons of Color

Blue skies hang high above the clouds
I feel joy when I rise in the morning
The rays of a beautiful sunshine
Lord, I embrace Your love
When the stars twinkle
I smile because I can see it
My spirit is alive to receive
When the wind blows I feel Your breath
I'm so mesmerized to discover
You seem to know what the soul needs
I welcome Your rainbows
When I pray I want to thank You even more
As the birds sing and whistle
You have an essence that speaks clear
When the dew in the morning greets You

CHAPTER 4

A Healing That Deserves Praise

I t seemed as if my life only consisted of sadness and pain. When my back was up against the wall, the fear and pain grew inside my soul. I never wanted to accept defeat, but my fears had me tossing and turning all through the night. I was hunted by thinking the worst in those times.

When things became overwhelming, I reached out to others for support. When they were quick to predict the worst outcome to my problems, I realized that I needed to be selective with whom I shared my situation. I suppose it's human nature to comment or give our opinions on matters. But just because a certain outcome resulted in someone else's life doesn't ensure that it will be the same for someone else.

Sometimes, depending on their responses, I felt worse. When I turned to prayer and the Bible for some hope and encouragement, I found a scripture that talked about having faith, and that's when I applied faith to the matter. It changed my perspective to believe that I would have a positive outcome. I remember being nervous because I had little faith. Somehow, I felt that I needed to have gigantic faith in order to get the results for which I prayed.

Today, my life exhibits a living testimony that my outcome was nothing like what I had feared most. I use to hear that I must have faith, but now I know what it entails. I endured an abusive marriage that went on for seventeen years, volatile dating relationships, being close to dying eleven times, being jobless numerous times, the loss of identity, and many superficial relationships that left me feeling abandon, sad, and broken. Since receiving God's healing and restoration, I am humble.

There is a God, and I am so thankful to my heavenly Father for chastising me to read His word for the wisdom and counsel that I needed. As I reflect, if it had not been for the hard times in my life, I wouldn't know how to stand or trust the power of God's word. My soul was weary, and I needed to see the manifestation of what His word declares. While I was going through adversities, God was forming a beautiful relationship with me. He strengthened my belief and gave me the victory each time.

There is a God who cares, and He's been so good to me. He's always there to wipe away my tears and knows how to bless me, even when I don't turn to Him right away. His mercies are new every morning; therefore, I am giving Him the glory, honor, and praise. My heart is filled with gratitude and my lips are full of praise as I delight in the things that remind me of His love.

Every Praise Is Heard

As I give thanks to You, heavenly Father
You have been better to me than I have to myself
Your love is so refreshing and everlasting
I thirst to be filled
Thank You for giving me a second chance
My heart longs to know You
I was lost in sin
You have blessed me through my prayers
Hallelujah, You've been so good
Sweet mercy and grace
Teach me how to love
Marvelous is what You are
When morning comes I will sing praises
I am drawn closer when I speak Your name
Faithful and true, I honor Your love

Breath of Heaven

While the storms were raging
My fears grew inside
Jesus, I need You, please save me
As the tears fell, You were there
By and by I made it through
Now the sun shines again
My life was spared by Your mercy
Lord, You came and rescued my soul
I give up all to follow You
When the wind blows upon me
I will look up to heaven
While my heart rejoices

Praise God
Hallelujah to King Jesus
My heart is full of joy and praise
Glory to my Lord for His mercies
I cannot find anything greater
I've searched and prayed
There is nothing like His joy on earth
I am thankful for my life
I raise my voice and sing
God's will be done in Jesus' name
As the angels spread their wings
I will lift my eyes and cry
The windows of heaven are open
Praises are flowing from my soul
While I express what I feel
Jesus, I love You

Prayer Birth Praise
When I pray my prayers
Lord, You know what's best
I want to give You the praise
When I tell You about my fears
Please give me the courage
I know that You're able
I honor You
Today is all that I have
Thank You for all of my blessings
Sometimes my flesh gets weak
There is victory in prayer
I will speak boldly and keep believing
While I give my praise
Oh Lord, shower Your glory
For all things are possible

A Beautiful Grace

Sometimes blessings are in disguise
Listen to the birds as they sing
Quiet your mind and ponder the sound
As seasons change and nature blooms
Peace and joy has filled the earth
And yet you are still here
Take the time to say thank you
Prayers are being answered
As you envision a different world
Your time will come to reap, too
Every living creature has a purpose
If you seek God's love you will find it
Believe in your inheritance and give praise
Stay steadfast in the Lord
His grace is unmerited and everlasting

Sing and Shout

I give honor to Jesus Christ as Lord
Praises shall flow out of my mouth
He's the head of my life, what a joy
There's no sweeter name that I know
I'm confessing to the world wherever I go
Oh what a friend I have till the end
My soul depends on You
Jesus, I am not ashamed to call Your name
There's joy and love in my praise
Shower me, Lord, with all Your mercies
I want to sing and shout
Hallelujah, sweet glory in Jesus' name

CHAPTER 5

Blowing Winds

As I recount the times when I was wandering aimlessly through life, the days were long and predictable. My dreams were many miles away as I pondered the way things were going in my life. I remember feeling excited when I was a teenager about becoming an actress, but the choices that I had made put me far from it.

While working countless temp jobs to help support my family, I was obligated. My life had formed around the lives of my husband and two sons at the time. I learned to adjust to the different roles that I had to perform daily: a wife, mother, provider, and maid. I decided to buy a planner so that I wouldn't forget appointments, deadlines, etc. The responsibilities grew as my family needs expanded.

The time when I would rise in the morning preparing for the day, I entertained many thoughts. I was losing myself to the daily demands of parenthood. I remember meeting a young woman on one of my temporary assignments who inspired me to go back to school for a degree. When I was alone, I started daydreaming about it.

In addition to contemplating school, my plate was completely full. But I felt like superwoman as I set out to pursue college. My drive was sincere as I exuded the passion that I needed to ignite the steps to becoming a college student. I felt empowered and excited about attending school. I felt even more excited after being awarded a scholarship and completing the first semester with a 4.0 GPA.

During my second semester, I found out that one of my close friends had passed away. I really felt sad, because I had recently sent her a letter to make amends for the reason I thought that we had grown apart. But after making contact with her family, they informed me that they had moved from where I sent the letter. While attending the funeral, I concluded that she probably never got the letter. Therefore, it was a closed chapter in my life.

Shortly after, I hit a brick wall when I realized that my personal life was falling apart. My marriage was heading for disaster, and the list was growing fast. I failed at concentrating on my studies, and my GPA dropped after I withdrew from a class. Eventually, the next step was I quit going to school. I panicked with feelings of defeat and anxiety. My hopes were fading, and my prayers were all that I had left.

I remember driving past a lake surrounded by homes. The landscaping was at its finest; it had a refreshment house, catch and release pond, water activities for small boats to sail, and an approximate two-mile walking trail that accommodated bikers and rollerblades.

The day that I felt completely hopeless, I visited the lake. As I walked along the trail, I looked up to the sky and the tears in my eyes begin to pour. I asked God to help me through it. It was too much to bear, because I was torn between two worlds.

The birds were flying in the air as the water moved slowly in the direction of the wind. I stopped to ponder the harmony and gazed into the faces of the other walkers. They seemed happy and cheerful as they strolled along. I was clueless in what direction I was going, because that was not my story.

It was obvious that my wheels were spinning out of control. As I took a deep breath to breathe, my thoughts became vivid. I meditated on freedom, good health, happiness, and love. I didn't think that much of it, because I liked the outdoors and being connected to nature.

I continued to go there just to pour out my heart to God; it went on for several years. The lake was my refuge; and it had an astounding effect on me. As my life changed, I walked right into the life I had envisioned the first time I heard nature's sounds of harmony at Lake Arlington.

Sudden Winds

No matter how things appear
I cannot give into my fears
For the Lord is with me
Trouble can not deter my hope
I have fought and struggled
As the days and nights fade
My heart believes
Although I am lost in the midst
My soul longs to be free
Each day that I ponder
I will hold to God's promises
The victory will come if I seek
I will continue to persevere
When the storm subsides
The sun will shine again
I will reap and rejoice
My tears will be for His glory
Victory will reveal the outcome

His Will

No matter where you are
You are safe in His will
If you have to cry go right ahead
If you have some bad news
Only God can change it
Trust in Him to guide your steps
The trials and tribulations will come
It is time to pray that Thy will be done
God has the answer to every problem
He's teaching mankind to depend on Him
Through faith we can make it
Run the race to the end
The safest place is in His will
It doesn't matter keep running
He'll be right there to embrace you

The Wind

When it moves it roams through the air
You can't see it, but you believe
Constantly reminded of how it feels
It is very real even when it stands still
It belongs to God and does His will
How can anyone be in doubt?
Everything that breathes lives
The word of God represents Him
His hand is upon everything
Joy comes to those who seek His will
No human understanding can imagine
How the wind looks, but we know it's there
To please God you must believe
The wind was created for His purpose
When God spoke the word

God's Spirit

Your love is endless
As it flows from heaven
Through the wind and rain
There's joy and love in the air
No matter how far away it seems
As You breathe life upon the earth
Every tear and prayer You know
Within the heart of man
Lies the secret to Your greatness
As You birth Your will
May the stars light the way
Through the rainbows and storms
Your grace reflects Your mercy
From sunrise to sunset You live
Breathing compassion upon the living

Favor

Doors are opening as I walk through
The windows of heaven are open to me
No time for doubting, my faith is real
Blessings are raining upon my life
I proclaim joy and victory as mine
Lord, I praise You for being so kind
Please hear the melodies in my heart
I am so grateful to learn about You
Thankful with every breath that I breathe
To God be all the glory above the stars
I see the twinkling in their eyes
When I close my mind to escape inside

Divine

Sweetly amazing how so
Your love fills the universe
Graciously as the wind blows
Life is where it all begins
Moments of an awakening
Bliss that transcends through time
Connecting righteousness to righteousness
Breakthroughs that are answered prayers
Miracles that affirm signs and wonders
A presence of peace and joy
To everything there's a reason
As the earth and stars rotate
Blessings are being manifest
Through tears, laughter, and praise
To every soul that believes
Windows are open in heaven
Faith unlocks the doors between both worlds
As divine order fulfills

CHAPTER 6

The Symphony

Before going to bed each night, I am reminded to say my prayers. There are so many things that I can talk to God about. I have been truly blessed to see some of the joys of life. The memories are like footprints on my heart. My spirit is calm, and I am open to receive the mysteries from up above.

I recall it was one summer's evening, when I left my bedroom window opened. I must have fallen into a deep sleep. While I slept, my soul must have been resting in the presence of angels. I heard chirping, whistling, and singing; it was supreme. As the pitch and sound elevated, I was awakened. I lay still in bed, but the sounds continued.

I looked over at my window as the sounds resonated inside my soul. It was around 5:00 a.m.; the birds were gathered together as they vocalized their praise. I was astounded by having the pleasure to witness how beautiful and heavenly it was. The symphony played on for close to an hour.

My heart was full of humility as I begin to whisper praises to God. I remember the time when I was down to my last; I had only seventy-five cents in my purse before payday. I was worried that I was not going to make it to the next payday. I prayed to the Lord, and then my thoughts shifted to the times when I was flat broke. But God was there, and He made a way for me through it all.

He blessed me with two high paying jobs that I was not qualified for according to having the required credentials. He saw my heart and opened many doors for me through working temp jobs. I had acquired many skills, and I was given favor.

On another occasion, I found a lump underneath my breast. When I noticed it, I didn't panic. I started praying to God and decreeing by His stripes I am healed. I placed all my energy and faith on prayer. I anointed myself with oil and continued to pray for my healing. But since it didn't go away, I had it surgically removed. The whole time I didn't fret or worry about the outcome, because I trusted God.

There was something else that distracted me, and that was my life's purpose. I have been consumed with inspiring others through my testimony. I am passionate about having a life with meaning and purpose for God. My hands are laboring for His goodness, and I know that He has my back, as long as I'm doing what pleases Him.

He is called faithful for setting the record straight. The Bible tells me that the birds do not worry about where they will lay their heads or what they will eat. He provides for them every day. I mean much more to Him than the birds. He never fails, and He's on time when I need Him.

Now I can see why the birds sing for Him and rise early. Their praise is heard in the heavens and the earth. Therefore, I too shall rise and honor my heavenly Father for being so gracious and kind to my soul. He holds my hand daily, angels are assigned to my side, and all the praises belong to Him.

Before I Rise

While I sleep through the night
I pray that my soul believes
Dreams are being born in the spirit
My life was created to prosper
As I draw closer to the Lord
I pray that He reveals a message
Sometimes the road seems dark
As I walk in the Spirit
I will trust in God's word
The answer will manifest
As I fill my heart with praise
For the birds of the air sing
As they rejoice and chirp
I to shall rise
While I witness God's blessings

Sound

Hearing God's voice through the birds
When they chirp and sing outside
Lets me know that I am loved
When I wake from the pouring rain
The heavens are telling all to rest
While God replenishes the earth
In the midst of His wonders and signs
I praise Him for such splendor
As whispers echo through the air
I have learned to listen and hold dear
My eyes are open
Life can be beautiful and sweet

Denise P. Ford

Warm Breeze
While a new season blooms
I'm fascinated to feel such warmth
As the sunlight shines upon my soul
Every breath that I take
I look toward heaven with praise
While my spirit seeks
The wind that blows to and fro
Sending messages through the birds
A harmony comprised of melodies
While they sing high and low
What a joyful day to witness
The beauty from a warm breeze

Arms Outstretched
No matter where you go
I will follow and protect you
I have the power to bring you through
My dear child, if you only knew
I have cried heavenly tears
You cannot understand My love
I am there to guide your every step
If you pray I will move
I am deeply and passionately concerned
Just look around and notice the birds
They neither sow nor reap
My angels are always on stand by
Fulfilling My command when I bless
I am never too busy and My arms are never too full
For they are always open to love you

The Birds

As I awake from the mysteries
I hear the birds singing and chirping
While the sun rises
On my knees I will pray
The sounds of such splendor
That comes to my windowpane
Once the day breaks they fly away
Free and above all to explore the world
Searching to find a nest for rest
Festive melodies of a joyful sound
How lonely life would be without the music
Rejoice to the beauty that is here
For God created all living creatures
Listen and have patience
As nature exudes God's goodness

If I

As the birds fly high
I too shall pray for grace
While I envision the wind
Up and away beyond the clouds
I will rest my weary soul
Praises shall flow like rain
Oh how sweet it is to dream
As the angels appear in the midst
Heaven is whispering my name
I believe if I can fly
While the music rings
My soul shall wonder
Sounds of praises are in the air
As the wind blows
Spreading the news all over the world

CHAPTER 7

A Substance of Hope

My creator, You have been my reason for living. All alone it has been You and Your Spirit that guides me. While I rested safely in Your arms, You clothed me with Your love, covering my being. What a beautiful place to rest my cares and concerns. I was born to depend on Your love and to seek Your will.

While I grow to understand Your word, there's a longing that tells me that You have everything. Where can I go from Your plan? Whatever I need, You are my source and strength. If I could see what lies ahead, I could courageously believe. Since having You for my anchor in life's storms, I have learned to turn to You. When the waves rise, I cry out to Your Spirit. Please help my soul hold fast to Your word, that You will never leave me nor forsake me.

Lord, You made me and know all my thoughts. Please take my hand, place it into Yours, and allow me to remember that secret place where I was born. What a joy to know that I was kept close. While being woven into Your image, I was knitted in Your core of greatness. Nothing is kept from You, because You created the darkness to obey Your command.

There was a time when my soul was shaken. I lost my parents to death, and my marriage was destroyed. While enduring my losses, I felt a part of me dying, too. The agony of finding the will to live was far from my reach. The highs and lows of putting things back together were daunting. There were not enough words of inspiration or encouragement to lift my spirits from day to day. When the phone calls became sporadic and the cards ceased, I felt completely alone. But through my tears and prayers, I soon found the strength to believe this too shall pass.

As seasons changed and I matured in reading the Bible, things did get better. My soul rejoices because I've seen the power of God move in my life. I honor Him for being my hope from where it all began. As I lift my head to praise Him, I count it all joy the good and the bad, because it is evident that without God, I am nothing alone.

Miracles That Birth Wings

When my heart is burdened
On my knees I will pray
Heavenly Father, I am in need
As I watch how the birds fly
I believe I can rise above
No matter what surrounds me
My spirit knows Your power
Yes, I have a friend in deed
Beyond the clouds, it's Jesus
I bless His name I give Him honor
While I walk this earthly plane
I won't give up until I'm free
Please lighten my yoke
I have the courage
Only You can answer my prayer

Honey Bee

As you labor to build God's kingdom
Know that your deeds are recorded
Heaven is smiling as you endure
Earth is not your final destination
The path may seem broad
Stay focus and keep persevering
Be about your Father's business
There will be times of testing
Hold onto God's unchanging hand
Life is preparation for eternity
Pursue harmony in all things
God's plan is bigger than you
Pray and keep seeking His goodness
As sweet as honey is to the bees
The Lord will cover you with His love
No matter how life stings
You will reap plenty of honey
Infinite grace, peace, joy, and love

Who Shall Abide

As your spirit lives
There is purpose for your life
Inside your soul lives another world
You must start preparing
As your body ages
Your spirit will grow
On the path to eternity there are mysteries
If you trust in God's plan
Your carnal mind will change
As you become aware of salvation
Start running the race
Be mindful when you are called
Keep praying to follow God's Spirit
Don't try to figure everything out
When it's time to end the journey
You don't have to wonder if you believed
As a reward to your faith
Your soul will reap eternal life

Grateful

I was lost in darkness
But You found me
Now I can see the truth
You never gave up
When the tears fell
I was blind by my flaws
Lord, I am forever thankful
You saw beyond my weary soul
You released the power
How can I ever forget Your love?
I no longer have to live in sin
I can make wiser choices and live
While I praise You through eternity
I beseech everything that You desire
For I know You are the messiah

Whispers

In my moment of happiness
I prayed from my heart
While the wind blew
My spirit was glowing from within
I looked up to the sky
Yes, another beautiful day
While caught in the moment
My tears fell
Christ died for my sins
I am blessed
My soul cried out the more
Today His grace fell upon me

Shame

Life does have its sorrow
Don't allow the enemy to close you up
God gave you a purpose
You don't have to be what you feel
Deliverance and joy is yours
Ask God to purge you
Sometimes we have to go through
Behind the sorrow there's a blessing
As you build courage, your morning will come
There's a reason for everything
For His mercy and grace abounds
Go forth, be bold, decree your healing

CHAPTER 8

Faithful and True

God, Your love is powerful and so amazing. I have searched high and low, but nothing compares. Lord, every word that You have written seems to apply to my being. There have been times when I've had to walk away from people, places, and things. I don't know how I made it through, but by grace I am able.

The day that I surrendered my fears, that's when things changed. In the past, I was clueless to who You were, but today I can proclaim a newfound faith. When I was walking in darkness, You were there. At times, when I would say my prayers, that's when I felt Your presence. Through those compelling moments, I realized that You are real. After every test, trial, and tribulation, there was a blessing waiting.

Now that my faith is stronger, I thank You for being true. Teach me how to love You and others. You are the air that I breathe, and my soul thirsts for more. There are some things that no one can explain or understand, but when I turn to You, I am certain that I am in good hands.

While I live to worship and give my praise, please help me. Please anoint my mind, body, and soul to prosper. Speak, Lord, to my spirit, so that my life may be a blessing to Your Kingdom. Let Your rain fall upon me, so I may receive peace, love, patience, meekness, forgiveness, grace, and Your mercy. Everything that I decree in Jesus' name, I believe. Every mountain that I have to climb, I am claiming the victory.

While preparing for my first sermon, "Live as You Are Called," I sought hard for spiritual direction. I went on the Daniel Fast, so I could gain strength and spiritual revelation that God was truly sanctioning me for the call. My heart and soul became discipline, as I prayed intensely while studying God's word.

The preparation process was incredible. While I prayed for someone to mentor me through it, that person never showed up. As the Lord saw my faith and heart, He began to show me in my dreams how He wanted to use me and which scriptures to study. I was compelled to following the process, while the signs and wonders were unfolding right in front of me.

The day I delivered my sermon, my faith and courage was astounding. When God summons you, be prepared to trust His way and lean not to your own understanding. There is no need to do anything else but obey, for He is faithful and true.

My previous prayers helped to prepare me, because I learned how to have a prayer life with God. His word gives life, and I am thankful that I am humble. My eyes were opened, and my heart was receptive to receive. When I sing praises, I am declaring His goodness.

Prince of Peace

You are the lily in the valley
God of my salvation to whom I behold
What a joy You give
An on-time God in the midst of trouble
I sing and shout about Your mercies
Victory is mine and that's my praise
Glory and grace, hallelujah
You gave me a second chance
I believe with all my heart
You are the God of all truth
I surrender and rest my life at Your feet
For beauty is Yours, my majesty

Truly Blessed

Where do I begin?
My mouth is full of praise
There's joy inside my heart
Heaven is smiling upon me
A new season has come
The sun is shining brightly
While I pause and breathe
My tears are pouring
As I sing of His goodness
Faith is golden
As I testify and witness
Miracles, signs, and wonders
While I prayed my way through
I concluded that I needed God
Quickly He moved heaven and earth
I could not have imagined
I can live and shout about Jesus
He lives so that I can believe

Unfailing Arms

I'm vulnerable and at Your mercy
There's joy inside my spirit
Your love has covered my faults
You are everything to my soul
When I was falling by the wayside
I fell into Your arms
I thank You, Lord, for Your love
I pray that Your grace covers me
When darkness falls
As my soul breathes for Your love
I've learned that there's protection
Your Spirit sees everything

A Blessed Beginning

As I pray for God's protection
My soul will stand still
While His angels cover my being
Dear Lord, there is evil lurking
I desire to please You
Speak, Lord, to my spirit
There are challenges that I fear
I pray that You cast Your light
You hold all the power in Your hand
Let Your glory reveal Your sovereignty
I will be still while You handle the matter
As I decree trouble won't last always
My day of rejoicing will come
As the tears fall, I must believe
No matter the outcome
I decree a feast of blessings
As I sit at the table before the angels
The toast will be in Your honor

You Bless

I am so thankful to serve You
A God who walks with me
Throughout the test of times
When I pray to Your Spirit
I am guided by the light
Your word abides with me
My soul is rejoicing
As You lead my spirit
The light is bright
What a joy I feel when I believe
Your mercies and blessings
Praise is in my heart
I am bound by grace
A beautiful gift to behold
May the glory be Yours forever

Sandals of Crucifixion

From the soles of my feet
I have loved unconditionally
Through the blood I live
My sandals were chosen
The word is bread to my spirit
I am called to bring God the glory
During the storms I became weak
I prayed to my Father
As He strengthened my faith
Crucified and resurrected
On the third day by His word
I no longer walk in the flesh
While I complete His will
May God's grace be with you
I sit on the throne
For I am born again through the Spirit
Heaven and earth have witnessed
The prophesy that was fulfilled

CHAPTER 9

Every Road Has a Journey

Sometimes it can be hard knowing which path to take, because every road leads to somewhere. The decisions and choices we make in life reveal who we are. There are many paths to take, however; if you think carefully you will have a desirable outcome. Some people choose not to look that far ahead. I caution you to choose carefully, because once you get started on your journey there will be many things that you will encounter and learn.

Life is a training course that teaches mankind how to live on earth. When you have dreams, goals, or a mission, it's very important to map out a plan on how you will get there. We are responsible for finding what route to take that will be suitable for our well being. Many distractions will come, and things will happen that will cause some ups and downs. Some roads are bumpy, painful, stormy, fast, slow, hard, or dark. If you find yourself going off course from your original plan, there is still time to change paths.

People will come to persuade you and speak things that are not conducive to your well being. Sometimes it's necessary to let people go their own way, if you are determined to reach your destiny. The reason so many people do not reach their destiny is they allow other people to travel with them on their journey. We get comfortable with having company and companionship, or find excuses to allow things to linger on.

God has everything set in motion to give you what you need to push you further. Don't waste another day sobbing over things that are holding you back. If you don't take heed, it could take years before you realize that you aren't on the path you started or decide to wait for others to see what you envisioned for your life. The things that you experience are reminders to teach you and to help develop you into becoming the person you truly are.

Therefore, keep pressing toward the life you want. Whatever you are seeking besides your dreams or goals, it's possible that it will show up on your path. Truly no one wants to be alone, but the solution to that is there will be new people that you will attract the closer you get to your goal. These people will have more in common with you, because we attract what we are putting out to the universe.

I recall taking many paths, running around in circles and back to start again. I wasted many years of my life, because I had no definite plans or goals. One day God stepped in and He spoke: "I will create in you a new spirit." Since that day my life was transitioned to a spiritual calling, and I have not looked back. I'm following the path that God planned for me. I'm walking through doors that I never fathom. I am thankful to God that I didn't miss the turn this time.

Sometimes we can miss the right turn, thus leading us down many roads in life. However, if you aimlessly wander around, you will end up on a road that can abort your dreams and destroy you as well. People sometimes forfeit their dreams, because they settle and do not know who they are. Do you know who you are?

Alone

The Lord made time for me
I was full of anger and baggage
My life was cluttered with others
As the seasons changed I looked around
There He was in the midst
I have learned to be alone and content
Although I am never alone
As the wind blows to and fro
He sends His angels to protect me

Wisdom

The Lord will give you wisdom
No textbook can teach you the mind of God
He imparts His Spirit into words
When in doubt seek the Lord for the answer
He brings forth the good out of all circumstances
Sit back and recollect the times when you were lost
God came through and showed you what you needed
He's wiser than any method of understanding
Sharper than any double-edged sword
A word from our majesty settles it
For wisdom is His and He grants the power
Pray to receive it, and don't be afraid to use it

Denise P. Ford

Seeking
What are you seeking?
Speak the words of blessings
Watch how they come
Your tongue carries the outcome
Be determined to reach high
The miracle is only a breath away
As your heart beats rapidly
The universe is forming your breakthrough
One by one your gifts are released
Fall to your knees with praise
Imagine how the stars light the sky
God's angels are descending
Bringing the good news
Walk into your abundance of joy
Cry aloud when your delivery comes

A Needy Soul
Two paths that crossed
As my heart feels compassion
I will never understand your grief
I pray that heaven is watching
While I stand in the midst
I will be that bridge that you need
There is a reason for everything
Life has seasons
You will get through it
As I impart words to your soul
I am petitioning a breakthrough
God can do the impossible
Your life has purpose, you must believe
Sometimes the road gets rough
It's only a test of faith
As I decree on your behalf
I speak the possible right now
Tomorrow will bring you happiness

Kindred Spirits

At times you will meet a stranger
Everything that happens is not by chance
As you smile and exchange dialogue
Your heart will begin to respond
As spirits connect
Be mindful of the light that shines
The road is narrow and long
As you travel day and night
An angel is there to assist
Sometimes you will walk alone
But know that God is present
Where there is worship and praise
Rejoice when that moment comes
As we entertain kindred spirits
God is revealing His love

Predestined

He knows my future when I pray
For my life was created for a purpose
I have surrendered to God's will
My steps are predestined
There's greatness in store
I shall see the truth if I seek
When I doubt the vision
I pray that my sins are forgiven
I will be mindful that God is with me
When I cannot see the light
I will be thankful and trust in Him
While I persevere towards greatness

CHAPTER 10

A Sinner's Prayer

When I asked God for His mercy to guide my soul, the tears poured from my heart. There was nothing more that I could do to change my life. I've always believed in prayer, but I was clueless at times if God was listening to me. I didn't pray daily, because I thought I was in control. Primarily, I was only concerned about making my life better. It was all about what I wanted, not what mattered the most.

When things turned upside down, I cried out for God's help. I was in trouble and afraid of the outcome. I humbled myself and prayed for God's mercy until He fixed the matter. The minute things were smooth, I wouldn't pray. The cycle went on for years.

One day I realized the reason I needed to pray daily. It was my conversation with God, and He was responding by allowing me to have breath in my body, peace of mind, food on the table, and clothes on my back and to overcome each obstacle that I faced whether good or bad.

He was teaching me that there is an invisible realm of the spirit where forces of good and evil operate. Since I can't see beyond my physical sight to the spiritual things, I can't fight with my bare hands or physical strength. This is the part that God handles in my life. He causes me to triumph over the evil that's trying to destroy me. My words are the prayers that activate Him to know that I need His protection and love.

I've always fallen short, because the struggles of life have gotten the best of me. I've had some good and bad days. I've been through the storms, but through it all I've learned to pray to the Master. He knows the sound of my voice and hears my feet running toward His word for safety.

While chastening me through my ignorance and pride, God was shaping my character and building a relationship with me through prayer. Now I know the power of prayer. I'm only able to go as far as my finite mind will allow me. My shortcomings have taught me that I need help, and God is the strength and source on which I depend.

I'm thankful to give thanks to God and express how I feel and what He's done for me. He is worthy to be given the time. I had to face it: if God can take time to put out my fires, and answer a sinner's prayer, He deserves more than a to-do list. He doesn't have to wonder if I have learned what prayer means, because I've surrendered my heart to Him.

Sinful Desires

Cleanse my soul, oh Lord
As I confess to You
Draw my spirit to repentance
Please forgive my actions
For my flesh has risen
When I stray deny my steps
I hurt when I disappoint You
I have defiled my temple
Lord, please renew my spirit
Search my heart and draw near
When my lustful desires creep
Convict my soul as You see fit

Did Heaven Say No

Without hope and dreams
My life is only a vapor
While I live to see the end
Sunrise to sunset
I will smile and forgive
For wisdom is precious
I have prayed a million words
Trust is important in every relationship
I've learned the value in living
The development of my character
What I say and how I live
Think it not strange
This yearning inside my soul
The inner voice that I hear
Words of love, grace, and redemption
If I never fulfill my greatest dream
I have lived it through my prayers
As I envisioned my life on earth

Bitter Tears

When life hurts the most
There's only one avenue
Turn to Jesus in prayer
Today is all that you have
Meditate if you will on courage
It's possible that joy is coming
You will not always get your way
Sometimes the bitter comes first
As you go through each test
Remember as the sun rises
This too shall pass
Your fruit will become sweeter
Casting away yesterday's sorrow
As you reflect and give God the praise
For God keeps all His promises

A Sinner's Heart

My spirit is searching
My carnal mind cannot fathom understanding
But through the blood I have another chance
I have fallen short according to my sins
Over and over I must admit
My heart will never be perfect
Even when I learn the lesson
Something new appears to test my faith
I must confess that I am a sinner
Standing in the need for prayer
God has a plan for my life
While I serve Him on earth

My Prayer

Bless my soul, oh Lord, when I pray
I beseech Your love for the rest of my days
I envision Your blessings upon my life
You are the only one who saves
I run from evil because You love me
It hurts my spirit to disappoint You
Jesus, I'm meditating on Your word
I ponder the goodness
As I petition my request
My faith is real
Ask, seek, and knock with all my heart
The glory belongs to Christ

Broken Vessel

Inside my soul there's hurt and pain
I can't continue living this way
Lord, I want that happiness that You speak of
I'm only human and I'm trying to understand
You have the power to fix the brokenness
I'm wounded from the troubles of the world
My temple is frail
I need Your love and mercy
If You can see while I pray
I know that You have the power
Please let me live again to make a change
I want to walk the streets of glory
I am a warrior, I just need Your strength
I pray that You restore me
While I fight the good fight

CHAPTER 11

Happiness

If you are in a place of peace and have understanding, what you have is invaluable. Whatever you may be thinking or feeling concerning the life you desire to have, it is within reach. However, it will take work on your part to change things.

The first step starts with putting your trust in God. It's not an easy thing to do when you are used to doing things your way. There isn't anything that we do alone without grace and mercy; sometimes we may not care to think so. The blessings, riches, health, and peace we possess on earth are treasures from God. He is good, and He loves you. There is no debate for those who love Him.

Some people have defined happiness by the external things that they possess, i.e. money, cars, homes, yachts, power, health, and wealth. We tend to paint a picture of these things in our minds as we envision happiness. If that were the true meaning of happiness, our houses would be full and our souls empty.

As we learn what is good for the soul, it will enlighten us to believe that there is a spiritual part to our being. If we take the time out to listen to our hearts, we will start to respect what we already have internally and embrace who we are, and not place our happiness on the external things that we possess or value.

I recall the time when I defined my happiness based on what my peers had and wanted or by what the media portrayed. Everything that I received was a temporary sense of happiness, because I still felt dissatisfied. During one of my unselfish moments, I relinquished myself from what I thought was the picture of being happy. I stopped putting all my physical strength and time into the matter. I wrote down my list of the things that I desired. I placed the list inside my Bible, because I felt that's where I needed to start.

I decided to read what the Bible says regarding my soul and how I could find happiness. I spent days reading the Bible and other positive material. I became interested in doing things that did not require spending money. I started to realize that I was alone more since I wasn't spending much. I believed that there was a change taking place, because I didn't feel a sense of hurry. I felt calm and at peace with myself, which caused me to love others and myself.

There are two paths to happiness that will cost you something. On one road you will need faith and God, and the other road currency. However, gaining material things looks appealing and sounds good. The more you have, the more you want, but after a while it can strip the soul from having inner peace and contentment that keeps us grounded and humbled.

I didn't know it at the time, but I was walking by faith. The spiritual law is true, "Faith is the substance of things hoped for the evidence of things unseen." We walk by faith and not by sight, and faith without works is dead. If we allow God to define what is best for us, we must turn to Him with our trust, take His direction, and walk the journey by faith. I am a living witness that He adds no sorrow to your blessings.

The Treasure Box

Lord, I believe Your promises
I thank You now while I'm here on earth
Praises are flowing from my heart
I can truly see how beautiful You are
My soul cannot fathom Your face
I know that Your word reveals who You are
For You have written many scriptures
I do believe that You will fulfill
You have done a priceless deed for my life
I belong to You, for my soul knows it well
My spirit is willing, and I cry out to You
Joy is in my heart because of Your love
For You know the box that You have for me
It behold the treasures inside
Every promise that You've set aside

Pearls of Grace

There are treasures in My heart
If you seek My kingdom, righteousness will follow
All of the riches that I behold from the heavens above
Pearls are priceless for they are hard to find
As you persevere, My grace is sufficient
I will provide all that you need
Let no one deter you from your path
Sometimes you will doubt, but don't give up
I am watching over your life with angels of mercy
As you get closer, I will share My possessions
I will uncover the silver and gold that leads to My Spirit
Where My pearls are stored

Denise P. Ford

Coat of Colors
While I wear my shield of armor
I will pray and obey God's word
As my Lord and Savior leads
My steps are predestined
I have been chosen to prosper
While I do my Father's will
On earth and in heaven
I will exhibit courage
Blessed and highly favored
Through the dreams He speaks
Heaven is on my side
When I rise I am protected
I will face life's challenges
Perseverance and faith to the end
When I stumble, Lord, catch me
I am walking in the anointing
My soul is covered and dipped
God is my shield and protector

Hallelujah, He's Worthy
God of the air that I breathe
God of my soul I thirst
My spirit abides with You
Hallelujah, You are my joy
In the morning I open my mouth
Praise is given to You most high
I have never gone without
Jesus, Your name is the sweetest
I call upon You
Signs and wonders follow Your word
The victory is already won

An Acre

Put God first in all that you do
Keep praying for your harvest to prosper
The seeds of your life will bloom
Some seeds were planted in your heart
Hold fast to your faith
The harvest will be plentiful
On the day of reaping
Endless fruit will be everywhere
As you stand in your own field of diamonds
Your baskets will be filled and overflowing
The treasures of your heart will be awarded
To God be all the glory from whom all blessings flow

One Sweet Day

Glory and mercy will surround my soul
My spirit shall sing and rejoice to the Lord
On that special day that He has planned
Oh how amazing it will be
There's no greater joy than the moment
When the tears fall
While the angels sit near
My soul will stand still
His grace will fill me
Lord, You are mighty and You live
I'm overwhelmed by Your glory
My heart adores You

CHAPTER 12

God's Child

No matter what you are up against, please believe that you are a child of God. Take a moment and think about your life, who made you, and why are you here on earth. At times, when we feel alone, having thoughts that no one loves us or understands the way we feel, we are quick to forget that there is someone else working behind the scenes on our behalf—God.

When I look back over the many trials, tests, and tribulations that I encountered, I can attest that God had His hand over my life. I can clearly see that life is about growing and learning. Lessons and various tests are placed in our paths to help us build character. As we're taught how to care for ourselves, make a living, or set out to venture a career, we are not aware that there will be character shaping along the journey.

Everything that I went through has been the catalyst to cause me to triumph, as I gained the hope to reach high for the dreams that were buried inside. Today, I'm living the life that God intended for me, as I witness how amazing it is that each day and season unfolds blessings that I never fathom. You see, there were many nights of crying, as I struggled in agony. When I couldn't cry anymore, I became stronger. When I had to face new challenges and obstacles, I held on to my faith. God was doing something within my soul to reveal that the pain will not hinder me or deter me away from the plans that He has for me.

It was through my suffering that I realized there was someone working on my behalf to cause me to triumph. There were times I couldn't pay rent, bills were past due, not enough money to cover major expenses, little food to eat, broken relationships, etc. I was a chronic worrier, and through it I became exhausted and sick. I learned how to pray consistently, as I shared my innermost fears with God. Somehow, I can't recall when, but He calmed my fears, wiped the tears, and gave me a peace within to believe that He lives.

Wherever you are today in your life, please believe that you are a child of a living God. Think and speak positive words every day and watch how your life changes. The Bible tells us that weeping may endure for a night, but joy will come in the morning. "Please remember that your morning is promised, all you have to do is keep your mind free of negativity and believe that God is doing a work in your life." Please share your testimony, because you never know how worse someone else has it. Remember to declare that you are a child of God and walk into the plan He has for your life. Blessings!

Everlasting Love

Your well never runs dry
I'm an empty vessel with a soul
Lord, please keep loving me
I'm hungry for Your mercies
You are rich with everything
I need an everlasting love
Anchored in Christ Jesus
An eternal unconditional love
Please hear my cry
Give me patience to hold on
I'm Your child, and I praise You
For You made me this way

As One

The day I enter heaven
I will sing to the heavens
While the angels lead
Lord, please bless my voice
When I open my mouth
For my soul knows Your love
Tears will fall like rain
I'll be in tune with every note
Oh joy, sweet joy from above
My prayers will manifest
God's written words
As my soul sings in harmony
Surrender it all to Jesus
My praise won't stop
Mountains are movable; He lives

Precious One

Listen to Me for I am there
Cast your burdens on Me
I AM the Great I AM
I send you sunshine to brighten your day
The birds come to bring you cheer
They sing and chirp to show their praise
I send My joy, will you believe
You are Mine, oh precious one
I will not deny My love for you
Please pray to Me, I want to fulfill
I will replenish your strength
You are a reflection of My love

Flowers by the Wayside

I love you with all My heart
If only you knew the depth
On the cross I gave you My life
It grieves My Spirit to see you in pain
Pray to Me, I am near
Read My word to seek My will
If you cry out
I have grace and love
I will restore your life
Don't just lie there in misery
You must activate faith to find Me
I created you with a purpose
You have a chance to shine bright
As I send you My word and the sun
Lift up your head and give Me the praise
I will strengthen your soul
As you gain the assurance that you need
If you show Me that you believe

Talk to Me

Are you lonely?
I am there inside you
I am sharing the warmth of My touch
Are you thirsty? I have water
Drink from My word
Put it to test and see My power I AM I AM
I created your heart, and I know everything
Please talk to Me, I am listening
The thoughts of My heart are like treasures
I want to love you endlessly
Please understand that I adore you

God's Child

Your spirit is sweet and pure
I love the way heaven made you
God has covered your soul in love
Keep smiling and reaching high
You were born to be great
Heaven is watching over your life
Let nothing deter you
As you build a relationship with Christ
Your star will shine bright
Stay on the path to righteousness
You were born to stand alone
Let your light so shine
Always remember these words of faith
Your soul belongs to Jesus
You were born to soar in His grace

CHAPTER 13

You Are Beautiful

Sometimes life can throw a curve ball your way. It can be very hard to see the next step. It doesn't matter where you start out; it's where you end up in life that truly matters most. Whatever you have endured, no matter how much pain you have carried, there is hope. There are tests that come to challenge you, to teach, inspire, and enlighten you.

As I struggled through the years of hurt, pain, betrayal, and trauma, I will never forget the days. I vented, cried, and wallowed into the wee hours of the night. The pain was so excruciating at times that I didn't even care who knew my business. I found someone to tell little by little of what I was going through. Somehow, I started to feel relieved as I felt a glimmer of hope, but then there were times when I felt like a fool for revealing the truth of what my life was like behind the mask. There was no one in whom I felt that I could trust with the fear of being embarrassed, ashamed, or rejected by others. I'll tell you it was a miserable and lonely place to be.

I was shaped by the unfortunate circumstances of my childhood, as it followed me into my adult life. I was surrounded by dysfunctional parents who suffered from alcohol, drug use, violence, and poverty. However, I was able to see the cause and effect that it had on their lives at an early age. As I learned to cope by escaping mentally through dreaming of being an actress, song writer, or author, my life journey has taken me on an emotional roller coaster. Then, I fell in love and married my high school sweetheart. As the cords of deception, alcohol, infidelity, manipulation, and domestic abuse unraveled, I hit rock bottom.

I fought mentally, spiritually, physically, and emotionally to regain the strength to live again. Today, I'm wiser, stronger, and living in the light. I am no longer in bondage or held back from the obstacles of the past. I am living on purpose, and my wings are certainly moving graciously as I envision the sun shining every day on my life. It feels marvelous to sing, smile, and embrace laughter. I am free to be who I'm destined to be my true self—beautiful. I attribute my gratitude and new life to God for hearing my prayers.

Please keep believing in yourself and never give up. There's purpose in all that you go through. It's not in vain; learn the lesson and pass the test. Remember that there is something beautiful about you as you embrace your journey.

Shower Your Glory

Sweet blessings that rain from above
To whom the glory belongs
My soul breathes
Like honey dew in the morning
I will give my praise
Your majesty of righteousness
As the wind blows at Your command
I'll sing the melodies that You send
My spirit will rise with grace
As You fill my soul with love
You are beautiful and holy
Like an endless waterfall
My heart feels Your touch
Holy Spirit, Your power is overwhelming
Let it pour as I shout about heaven
Lord, have mercy
My lips are overflowing with praise
As You wash my sins away

Wither

A beautiful flower yet slowly fading
The youth of my soul is crying
Day by day I feel the changes
What's here today can be gone tomorrow
Nothing lasts forever, no matter what it is
The sun shines to absorb my smile
While I live to grow on the journey
Loneliness has sat in to claim its place
Precious memories to behold
For time is not on my side
Blessings of love rain from above
By allowing my soul to breathe

Adore
Lord, breathe Your breath on me
Like a ray of colors to be sung
My heart is open to receive
A breath of melodies
Your presence is bliss
Mercy, sweet mercy
While my thoughts are forming images
My soul hungers
Truly You are my gift of hope
A breath of melodies
My heart longs for joy
Oh mercy, sweet mercy
Thank You for Your love
Let it rain, let it rain
Your love is truly amazing

A Beautiful Blessing
Beautiful lady, where did you come from?
You must be an angel
Where did you leave your wings?
Your aroma and spirit is sweet like Jesus
Beautiful lady, that's what you are
I thank the Lord for sending you into my life
As God pours His grace and mercy upon you
I can feel your praying spirit rise
Everything about you seems heavenly made
My soul rejoices to see God's gift inside you
Beautiful lady, you are filled with heaven's delight
You have been blessed and anointed to soar high

Mountains Are Movable
As the Lord shows His mercy
Walk in faith for what you believe
You were chosen to stand on mountains
Pray to the Lord daily
Miracles will unfold before your eyes
Keep seeking His righteousness
Your life will bring God the glory
It is His desire to bless you
Pour out your heart with praise
Know that you are loved
Decree a ministry in Jesus' name
Show God you are serious
Keep petitioning your prayers
You are called to be victorious
Right now I speak blessings into your life

Arise
You will live a long life
Your wings will grow strong
No storm will destroy you
The fire may come
Have no fear in the things that you see
Don't listen to negativity
You must run and not give up
The power of the Lord is with you
Conquering all obstacles
As you walk with the Lord
He is shining His light of victory
You will triumph over your enemies
Always remember your lineage
You are a joint heir with Jesus
His grace and blood covers you
When you fall down get back up
Call on the name of Jesus
For it is your inheritance

CHAPTER 14

Heavy Laden

My daughter, there's nothing that I can't feel and there's nothing I can't see. I know the pain that you carry in your heart. Please read the Holy Bible. I come to give you rest. I am a Spirit that you cannot see with your physical eyes. If you take up My word and read it daily, I will reveal the mysteries to your heart.

You were placed on earth to complete your assignment. I have given you a purpose to fulfill while you labor during the journey. If you ask, seek, and knock, I will answer. I've placed the tests, trials, and tribulations upon your path. Just look around and ponder about your life. I've brought you out; unfortunately, many didn't make it through. It does not matter what decisions or mistakes you've made. I knew all about the things that you were going to do before you knew it. Don't be so hard on yourself; if you have to cry, let the tears fall.

I come to bring you healing, deliverance, love, and joy. You can't see all of the promises that I have for you, because they're in the spirit realm. In order to activate what I have for you, please yield to My call. I have plenty of grace to bring you out of that bondage. Don't be concerned about what the world thinks of you. I created you, and you are my work of art. I love what the world discards; just come and surrender to My will.

Whatever is troubling you today, give it to Me through your prayers. I want the best for you, and I want you to shine. I've placed a light inside your soul to guide you through. If you take heed and learn about Me, you will begin to walk towards the light. Nobody's perfect, no matter what you see. Some people are professionals when it comes down to wearing a mask. I love everything about you whether it's your smile, your spirit, or your brokenness. I can restore you and make you whole to walk in holiness. I fashioned you out of mercy and grace.

As I impart my love into your vessel, I want the glory and the praise. You must come out of that lonely place and ask for My hand. I have placed angels on your paths to assist you. When you are born into the world, you are blind until you realize that you can't make it on your own. When you realize that you can't handle the thorns, that's when I draw near—to dry the tears from your eyes and give you new life.

If you believe, I will send you signs and wonders to show mercy. I am love, and all the power is in My hand. Release the hurt and embrace the people I've sent to show you the way. I'm watching over your life, and I'm hoping you believe that I am a mysterious God and I am where My word and love abides. Come if you need rest from all the troubles and disappointments of the world. If you make one step, I'll carry you as you grow in My word. At times when you are weak or if you should grow weary, I will be there to strengthen you.

The world will not tell you that you need My word. I want you to reach your destination. I am sparing your life, because you mean more to Me than you will ever know. I have plans for your soul. As your soul prospers, you will fulfill the work that I have started in you. Remember I do not see you as the world sees you. Will you come?

No Compromising

From the womb I shaped you
Before you grew to know Me
My son Jesus bore your iniquities
Nothing has changed My plans
Stop looking back and reach forward
Lift your arms and embrace your destiny
Inside your soul I will birth My glory
Let the cleansing go forth
I've chosen you to walk the walk
Don't try to figure things out
As you cry let the tears fall
I am strengthening you to stand tall
I AM I AM the living God
I have given you all that you need
I come to give you new life
My daughter, I am pleased
My eyes are watching over you
Now walk with Me

A Breath Away

Today may be my last
As You breathe upon me
My eyes are filled with tears
Dear Lord, I love You
You are that burning light
In heaven and on earth
I need a sweet melody
While I have the chance
Once again with honor and praise
Sweet eternal light of glory
Bless my soul today
If I should depart this life
Rest my soul in Your presence
As I take my last breath
While I sing how I love You

A Pebble in the Sand

Like treasures buried below the sea
You cannot attain unless you seek
The value is high and worth millions
Life can be beautiful if you believe
Dreams do come true
Continue to pray for what you desire
There will be times when darkness falls
Trust in God and His word
For the sun will shine again
As the light shines upon the earth
You will find that unquenchable
Whatsoever you sow
Bask in the moment if you will
Rejoice and sing praises
Heaven has a plan for your life
Like pebbles in the sand
You will find your treasures
When you seek God's unconditional love

Silent Prayers

When I cannot see Your plan
On my knees I will pray
Bless my soul, oh Lord
For my mind is consumed
There are many distractions
Whisper a word to my spirit
While my soul waits
Restore the things I need
My praise needs mercy
Pour Your grace upon me
Send Your blessings on earth
That I may rejoice when I wake

The Words in the Mirror

Within my soul, there are hidden words
As I walk the journey, they seem to appear
Watching and directing the steps that I should take
Sometimes it's hard to look within for such fear
I might not be able to accept the challenges
If I can only believe and walk by faith
I will be able to have the courage to listen
There's an audible voice that I hear
When things are quiet and I'm alone
My heavenly Father abides
Helping me to make the right steps
While I follow His word and Spirit

Soul and Spirit

As my flesh dies daily
I will read God's word
While I live my life on earth
As I look at my surroundings
I've placed my time on petty things
For the word is my nourishment
I've come to understand there's more
If I continue to turn the pages
My wisdom will increase and enrich
Now I know the difference
There's an abundant life with Christ
Through the blood, Spirit, and water baptism
The outcome will give Him the glory
As my soul prospers in all things
While I submit to doing His will

CHAPTER 15

There is Room for Error

Tere will be times in our lives when we will fall short, no matter how much we may want to please someone. Please understand that we serve a God who loves us unconditionally. You don't have to wear a mask or behave differently.

Put God first on your list and ask Him to help you find order. Learn to prioritize your daily tasks. Having a prayer life, studying the word, and developing an intimate relationship with God is crucial. When you put these into practice, you will understand the importance of people pleasing. You were created to worship, fellowship, and praise God. People can run around and beat themselves up with trying to buy love and acceptance.

As you grow in your walk with the Lord, He will reveal the important things that truly matter. When we understand that we are only human and there is room for error, we learn to love God first and secondly love our neighbor as ourselves. Life is passing by when we have disputes with each other, ask God for discernment, and be willing to forgive. We all make mistakes and have shortcomings. If someone is angry, jealous, envious, or unforgiving, you must take it to God.

As you live on, you will see that it isn't important to people please; be about your Father's business. Hold no grudges in your heart and continue to smile and love. Everyone is not on the same level in Christ. Many are called, but few are chosen. You must get yourself in order to be ready when God calls. Allow God to teach you how to apply wisdom and knowledge. If you yield to His word, you will prosper. When we don't follow God's plan, we always fall short and remain unfulfilled.

As we face the truth, sometimes we can never resolve the matter. So discern that God is concerned about your heart. Stop wasting time on the past and know that God is the only one to define your mistakes and validate your human errors. If He is pleased with you, that's all that matters.

Falling Leaves

While I stand in the midst
I will slowly breathe
As my heart captures the essence
There are many rays of splendor
While nature blooms in its season
How sweet the sound
As the wind blows, time is passing
Therefore I must pray
While the birds sing
One by one the leaves are changing
As they cover their branches
Swiftly they scatter as they fall
My soul is in awe
As God reveals His glory
Whispers of praise when we pray

Praying Spirit

Holy Spirit please rain down
Hear my prayer and direct my steps
I want to know You
When I'm afraid I need to believe
My faith is always being tested
The Lord is mighty good to me
I'm asking for mercy
Lord, You sent Your Holy Spirit to guide me
I'm praying to receive Him fervently
While I build a relationship
I won't live a day without saying thank You
Let it rain when I go into my prayer closet

Sleeping

God, give me peace and sweet dreams
Let my thoughts escape this world
For I am weighed down
If I can visit You for only a minute
Please allow me the chance
Take me into that place that I ponder
I'll promise not to pout
By the break of dawn the birds will be singing
While the sun rises in the east
If You should decide to send me back
While blowing breath into my nostrils
I will never forget Your love

Melodies from Heaven

Words are powerful if you believe
God knew how to express His love
When He decided to create
The heavens and earth were formed
By spoken words from our creator
As He imparted His Spirit into words
Life was being birth out of His voice
Nature took place to bear fruit
While the birds chirped and the owls listened
Today we sing, dance, and live by words
The mind sows and the heart reaps
The written words from above
As you grow and learn about God
The Lord will reveal His mysteries
Through the melodies from His heart

The Trees

They stand side by side and sometimes afar
Each having its own beauty and size
Amazingly distinctive in appearance
A tree that stands on good ground
Bears good and prosperous fruit
It has the victory to endure and produce
Yet a tree that wavers bears sparingly
We know it by its fruit
It cannot withstand the storms of life
For God knew its purpose on earth
He that is strong and rooted in the word
Shall be planted like a tree by living waters
As the winds blow you may bend
Good fruit will still spring forth
If you are ever weak or in doubt
Christ is the vine that sustains the root

Forgiveness

Nobody's perfect, mistakes are made
If you ask for forgiveness, mean it
No matter what it is, make the step
Jesus commands us to forgive
We must learn how to treat one another
When we hold back, our blessings are hindered
The baggage can get heavy
There are lessons that we have to learn
We are all human trying to live on earth
God knows why He instructs us to forgive
Don't wait till it's too late to let someone know
Pray against the spirit of pride
Free yourself and move forward
Blessings come to those who obey God's will

CHAPTER 16

The Blood Never Expires

We have witnessed that the journey does get rough. Sometimes you may think that you are progressing and out of nowhere you're faced with a trial, test, or tribulation. You must realize that no matter how you got there, God is a Master in all storms. Hold on as you go through it. Don't give up or go by what it looks like. Seek the Lord with all your heart, mind, and strength.

There is good news that you can make it when trouble comes. In order to get the victory in Christ Jesus, you will need to access to some spiritual tools. You will need the word of God, faith as your insurance card, continual fasting, prayer, and true worship as you persevere. God wants to teach you how to walk in the Spirit as He teaches us in His word. If you believe, you will get the victory and come out of every mess or storm being able to give God the glory and praise. He is a Spirit whom we worship in Spirit and truth. How else are we able to witness more effectively to the world that He lives?

Therefore, know that every one of your steps have been ordered; everything that happens to you is predestined and there is a reason and a significant purpose. God is trying to perfect some things in you. He wants to mold you out of greatness. But in order to accomplish the best results, sometimes we will be placed into the furnace. It's very frightening and difficult to see the end as a victorious outcome. But as you persevere and have a determined mind and do not quit under any circumstances, you have already shown God that you accept His good and perfect will. He loves you and wants to prosper your soul. God is seeking the pure at heart who love Him to go out on the battlefield to slay the enemy. It takes perseverance, character, and hope to endure the tests. He will walk you through it and guide you to safety.

You see, Jesus knows that the enemy is trespassing when he is lurking near one of God's beloved. As children of a living King, we must be aware and know that everything is about principalities of darkness that wait in the spirit realm. As you study and learn the word of God, you will begin to see the fruit of your labor. You will be better equipped to withstand the forces and snares of the enemy.

Whenever you feel that you're not worthy or good enough to be used by God because you have sinned or have sin in your life, fall down on your knees and repent and thank Him for the blood. It does not matter what you've done as long as you know who you are in Christ Jesus.

Most importantly, remember what Jesus did for you on the day that He died on the cross. He rose three days later to demonstrate to the world what no man could have ever endured. So remember to pick up your Bible and start walking, living, and talking about the good news of the gospel. Once you have witnessed the power of the resurrected blood working in your life, you will never be the same. Whatsoever Jesus sanctions, redeem, restores, and resurrects has been paid in full through the crucifixion that shed His blood.

Wings from Heaven

Breathe on me, dear Lord
Spread my wings
My faith is all that I have
Please guide the way
Teach me where to go
I know there's a secret place
When the storm comes
Send Your angels to cover me
I believe in the impossible
For You created the universe
I need Your hand for refuge
As the angels fly by my side, hold my hand
My heart longs to know You
Heaven, I am ready to fly

Spirit of Praise

While resting my thoughts
There is an inner voice that whispers
Hallelujah, grace, and mercy
My spirit calls upon His name
Sweet Holy Spirit let it rain
I'm captivated by such essence
While my heart is fluttering
I will pray Your will be done
I trust Your Spirit to guide me
Please fill my soul, Lord, with love
Let my praise be filled with honoring You

The Watchman
Time is a precious gift
What are you doing with your life?
The deeds that you sow will be revealed
There's no need to look back
As you mature to understand why
You cannot undo what has been done
Pray to the Master above
Ask, seek, and knock
There's a calling on your life
Don't wait for trouble to find you
Learn to love and serve
As you grow, your garden will prosper
There is someone that sees everything
If you keep your eyes on God
You will have a fulfilling life
Eternal blessings will come
To every man that lives
He who keeps his eyes on God

Breath of Will
My life and trust is in God's hands
As You breathe breath into my nostrils
I only have today to give my praise
For tomorrow is not promised to be mine
Lord, I love You and I pray to walk righteously
While I honor You with my life
The moment I wake please draw near
I am thankful to know what's important
As I prepare to read Your word
My faith is anchored in Christ
When You move through me, I will bow
My greatest desire is to abide in Your will

Offering

Today I will give You my praise
Dear Lord, I honor Your name
Jesus, You are the sweetest
Thank You for everything
I surrender my time and labor
As I seek Your kingdom
When I look around I am blessed
I cannot help but fall at Your feet
Your love and protection keeps me
Through the rain and storm
I have been restored and redeemed
I know of no other source
Lord, I am offering to You
Everything that I thought I wanted
As Your glory rains upon me
Favor and grace belongs to You
Jesus, I surrender all
As an eternal offering I submit my heart

The Fire Inside

As I petition my prayers
Divine order is forming
While my soul listens to the universe
Whispers of praise
Messages of love and peace
My future will be fruitful
Hope and prosperity shall never depart
While I decree miracles
As the day comes to an end
The power will manifest
God's blessings and truth
My praise will be glorious

CHAPTER 17

A Thankful Praise

As the sun shines upon my face, I can feel an essence of love. Today, I am still alive and here to say thank You. God, You are truly amazing in all of Your wonder, brilliance, and love. I can attest to what it feels like to cry, when there is no one to lean on. As I stand and testify to the world, shine Your light upon me. My spirit fears You and knows Your power.

I am able to live a better life, because Your Spirit never left me. I would have never known You, if I had never been down. There were times when I couldn't see my way, and I had no clue which way to go. Things started to make sense when I prayed and applied faith.

As I recount this, it only seems like yesterday when I didn't think I was going to see the blessings I have. I am compelled to love You more. I understand that my experiences alone could not have afforded me the favor, and anointing that's on my life. I am honored to praise You, because You are with me. I will witness to others about how good You are. There's no way I could hold back my praise, as I introduce You to others.

My brothers and sisters, if you have a need and are wondering how to get an answer, please muster the faith to believe there is someone who knows your name and everything about you. The Lord is preparing someone to bless you.

I am only a vessel being used to speak into your life. Stop where you are and sincerely say thank You to God. When praises go up, blessings come down.

There are so many things to begin with, if you have a willing heart to believe that you were created by God. The battle is already won; let your praise be heard. Sure, things aren't perfect, but that doesn't stop the new blessings from coming. Remember nothing happens by accident, when God is preparing a blessing for you. He moves by His own Spirit, when we believe. Decree your praise.

Unquenchable Joy

Oh my soul sings
Lord, what I'm trying to say is thank You
Truly my life was a mess until You blessed it
I'm so thankful that You looked down
You were right there while I was praying
I opened my mouth and called Your name
Jesus, You are so good to me
Oh the joy makes me cry
All things are possible if I believe
I'll sing Your name to the world
You have the power to heal the hurt
Thank You for changing my tears to joy

Piano Praise

Lord, as I play the keys on the piano
I'll pray to give You all of my praise
With each keystroke I'll move graciously
As I sing along to the melodies
What a joy I have inside my heart
I'm playing for You to see my praise
Tune after tune I can feel Your presence
Please be near as the tears fall
Oh my Lord, You are awesome to be praised
Hallelujah, sweet Jesus, I'll play
Teach me whatever You wish
My fingers will follow the keys to Your Spirit

A Soulful Hymn

My heart sings to the melodies
Lord, You are so sweet to me
My soul sings about Your peace
The more that I sing the deeper it feels
This is my tune that I hum to Jesus
I love You, what a friend
When I'm alone I open my mouth
Jesus, Jesus, Jesus, Jesus
You have never failed me, thank You
I sing this song from my soul
Peace and joy surrounds my life
Thank You for the joy I have found

It's Pouring

Your love is everlasting
I am mesmerized by all that You do
My eyes have seen miracles
Day by day as I witnessed
There is infinite power in prayer
While I count my many blessings
Lord, rain on my poor vessel
While I stand in the rain
It feels marvelous to sing
Oh my soul shall give You the praise
As it pours from heaven to earth
I cannot fathom anything greater
It's all divine, and through the blood
An endless love and grace
Heaven and earth beholds Your glory

A Promise

He reigns although you cannot see
When He whispers a word to your spirit know that it's real
There's nothing on earth that He gives then steals
He put it into your inner man to start the process
It was placed there as a deposit
His Spirit relates in the spirit for all things to prosper
Pray and believe that His word is true
He's an on-time God with loving grace
It takes a season or two for your breakthrough

Dancing Soul

As my soul rejoices I will dance
For my Lord, who watches above
I'm free to move in the Spirit
My arms are out stretched
Let Your Holy Spirit fall upon me
Around my soul while I dance
Joy is what I feel
As my cup runs over I cannot stop
For my praise is in my dance
Lord, to You my gift is pure
I thank You for entrusting me
Sweet mercy, I love You

CHAPTER 18

His Grace Found Me

Where do I begin with how good God is to me? My life was full of darkness for many years; the thoughts of suicide followed me. I didn't know how to get past the shame, guilt, and hurt. The way that I lived my life gave me no real joy. I blamed others and myself for the choices I made. I couldn't figure out why I was running around in circles and never able to find any peace.

Somehow, I concluded that my life was cursed, if I continued to live the way I had. I cried out to God for His mercy to show me a better way. While searching for change, I decided to live positively and treat others as I wish to be treated. I wanted to know what it felt like to be loved and respected. I no longer desired to be around the crowd with which I was running, because they would often remind me of the old me.

During my search, I started reading the Holy Bible faithfully and pray. The process humbled me to honor God. At first, I was confused about many things concerning the Bible. I bought Christian books that were scripture based to help my understanding. One day while reading the Holy Bible, things started to make sense. I received revelation knowledge about the scriptures. That's when I realized God was speaking to me. I rejoiced while giving God my time and praise. I was captivated by the way I felt over God's word. My heart was filled as the thirst continued.

The search became a part of my pursuit to happiness. The things I used to say and do because of the guilt was gone. My self-esteem was lifted when I turned to God. He revealed to me how much I am loved. I felt the love and closeness, because things were turning around for the better. I continued to worship and give praise daily. I had found someone who loved me as much as I needed. If I didn't know how deeply I needed God, I would have given up. Therefore, I gave Him my heart. My soul thirst for the joy He gives.

When the soul is filled with the peace of God, there is nothing to compare to it. The universe understands how to give praise through its purpose. My life was created to be a part of worship. God's grace follows me, as I diligently seek to please Him. Thus, if it hadn't been for the blood, my sins would have destroyed me. But by the grace of God, I am what I am. Christ saved me and enabled me through God's grace to tell the story of how I was lost, but now I'm found.

Fountain of Grace

My life was spared for Your glory
I have praises and thanks to give
Lord almighty, it's Your love
I don't deserve Your mercies
You loved me before I knew You
Please cover my soul
I am so thankful that You are a forgiving God
I could never repay You for my sins
For I am a sinner
Your grace redeemed me, Lord
I adore You for saving my life
Hallelujah, thank You Jesus, the blood lives

Glorious

I'm standing still in amazement
I can hardly breathe or exhale
My mind cannot gather enough words
God, I'm under the power of Your worship
I am trying to capture the moment
While my spirit rejoices
For my heart tells me that it's Your love
Yes, my eyes have seen the glory
There's nothing more beautiful
Our king, we honor
Your majesty of grace
That's what You are
Everything that's righteous and pure
I submissively obey Your written word
As I uplift Your name
Hallelujah, hallelujah, You are worthy

Holy Spirit

As my soul abides close to God's word
I pray to receive all His love
Some things are absolutely unforgettable
Breathtaking while I witness
I desire to be in Your presence
The joy that You give makes me cry
Sweet Holy Spirit, I welcome You
I praise God for sending You into my life
Your worth is more than millions
All the gold in the world doesn't compare
I lift my hands to give praise
While my spirit thirsts for Your blessings

Standing in the Rain

My heart is heavy
Lord, what are You saying?
I have prayed and fasted
I cannot seem to get things right
Time and time I've tried
Please feel my tears
I hope that You bless me
There's a melody that I hear
The storm won't last long
My emotions are broken
I need more of Your anointing
Cover my wounded soul
Please hear my prayers
I will stand in the rain
For my soul is thirsty for an answer

Cup of Grace

When I rise in the morning
I will praise You, for I am Yours
Lord, will You replenish my soul?
I need Your love and forgiveness
I pray that You send an angel
Watch over my portion
Please whisper to my spirit
While You pour, I won't hold back
I cannot fathom the taste
Your Spirit is the sweetest
When You bless have mercy
For I am an empty vessel
My heart is beating passionately
While You give a measure
My soul will sing Your praises

Wings of Grace

As I press forward
Through the rain and the storms
My soul will sing His praises
I'm decreeing my breakthrough
As I reach higher I won't stop
There's an abundance waiting
When the tears pour, I will cry
As I face each day
God is in charge, and I am His
Dear Lord, bless my soul
I don't have much time
Calm the rain and the storms
When I cannot see the light above
Speak life to my spirit
As I soar through the clouds

CHAPTER 19

Believing in You Makes the Difference

Sometimes it could take years before we can see what others see in us. We are born with a special unique gift or talent that identifies who we are apart from others. The hardest part about this is discovering what our gifts and talents are. It's an adventure trying to figure out why we are sent to earth.

The way that I see myself today was not how I perceived who I was thirty years ago. I've had to endure many storms and adversities. My life was volatile at times, with many uncertainties. The journey seemed endless. Many strangers came into my life and spoke kind words of inspiration and encouragement to me. Since my vision was blurry, I didn't understand it, but they saw something special in me. I had no clue or hint to what it could have been in what they were seeing.

I perceived who I was by the way I was treated and loved. I wore Goodwill clothes; I never had enough money to buy school items or lunch every day. When I got a new pair of shoes, I treasured them, and any piece of clothing for that matter. I desired to wear the cute ponytails and barrettes in my hair, but since I didn't get my hair combed often, I started combing it myself until it fell out. I didn't feel pretty most days.

I remember getting teased sometimes while growing up because of these things. That was the beginning to what caused me to think less of myself. I started harboring sad feelings and searched for others to like me. When my friendships didn't turn out as happy experiences, I felt even worse. Therefore, I climbed inside my shell.

As I grew into an adult, my low self-esteem followed me. My confidence about myself was shattered. The picture of who I was in my mind was a broken-spirited, timid woman. I acted very bashful, and I felt restricted. The person who I was created to be was buried behind the brokenness. It was a hard road to walk while trying to gain self respect and genuine love. I did have some sunny days that caused me to think about the dreams that lay dormant inside my heart. Those thoughts didn't last long, because I was not living as the person I was predestined to become.

The path that I took to get here has put me in a better place. This is what I have to say about the journey—believing in yourself makes the difference. When I encountered an awakening by God, that whole experience turned me around and pointed me in a new direction. Since learning how to love myself with God's help, the baggage has gotten lighter.

Now that I know my life purpose is advocating for women and children, I'm focused and my vision is clear. I can feel God's love covering me. If you have ever felt any of these emotions regarding self-love, esteem issues, it doesn't matter what others say about you, whether good or bad, because what truly matters is what you believe about you. If you want to be beautiful, loved, or free, it starts with you. Believing in yourself makes the difference.

Pray and learn to find ways of loving yourself, doing what you were made to do, and being the true you. There is something special that God has put inside each of us. Someone else has already been down the road you're traveling. It is not a coincidence that you are reading this, because God does use people to show how merciful and loving He is to all mankind.

The season of preparation comes before the caterpillar turns into a butterfly. The discovery process can be long, difficult, and excruciating. But in due season the world will see its beauty after the process. Now that it's your turn to let heaven's light shine bright upon the extraordinary you, remember: Believing in yourself makes the difference.

How So

Whatever you fear
I will be there to build your faith
I created you to prosper
Nothing will defeat My plan
I have covered you with My word
Read it to find your assurance
First you must surrender your desires
I know that you don't understand
I have ordained your tests and challenges
I am the light and the resurrection
I have every solution to what you need
Seasons are on time
Look at the forest that I have planted
Watch how the seasons change
I give you foliage and flowers
My hand is upon everything
When you come into this knowledge
I will fill you with My peace

Living Waters

My fears are only shadows
As I tread upon the earth
I will kneel and pray for the light
Jesus, I know You are the way
When trouble finds me I will stand
For my life depends on Your love
When darkness befalls my path
I will rejoice and sing praises
For I know Your eyes are everywhere
Birth Your word of truth when I call
There's no other name that I know
Sweet Jesus, that's who You are
While I stand at the bank
You are the Messiah of the living God
Let Your rivers flow
Send Your angels and doves over me
As I lift my hands towards heaven
I will be able to face the unknown

Denise P. Ford

Over Flow

While I stand in the midst
Dear Lord, please take this cup
The thorns of afflictions
I don't know where to go
Please hear my prayers
I need Your strength and grace
For I am bound by life's trouble
My flesh is tormented
Give me a fresh anointing
My faith is all that I have
No matter what happens
You are the ultimate source
Let Your joy fill my soul
As the tears fall from my heart
Rain on me till I'm made whole

Aspiring

Although my prayers are secrets
I will trust God in all things
As my soul rests in His care
While pondering success
As it rains from above
Tears of gratitude I release
As that season comes
Beautiful flowers are in bloom
Birds are flying near and far
While sweetness surrounds my being
Raindrops appear one by one
As I hold onto such images
Through every tear and struggle
God is awesome and trustworthy
Today I can attest that He lives

Lilies in the Morning

Amidst a blessing to behold
While listening to the wind
As my soul breathes
Echoes of soft whispers
As the pounding grows deeper
My mind slips away
Suddenly I remembered a melody
A peace that surpasses a season in time
As my heart wonders
A brighter day is in bloom
The dew in the morning
I too shall rise
Another world is forming
Far and near it greets
Merging two worlds as one

Healing Waters

My soul cries for rest
But I cannot find it
I pray God's will be done
I envision my spirit searching
Traveling high and low for refuge
Bless my soul, oh Lord
Replenish my faith while I believe
My soul needs healing
Send an angel to answer Your will
While I seek God's Kingdom
May Your peace rest upon me
I will be planted like a tree
Resting by the rivers of living waters
My spirit will bow to thank You
While I give You my praise

CHAPTER 20

My Story

When I hit a brick wall, everything in my life crumbled. I had lost everything, and I wanted to die. The day God spoke to my spirit, He changed me. I learned to put my trust in Him completely. The life that I had lived was tumultuous. I had no clue that I was in a spiritual war. My soul was weary, because I felt defeated by the struggles of life. Through the difficult times I searched for relief by reaching out to spiritually seasoned ministers. I was tired of running around in circles, but at that point I had hit a wall.

I asked for prayer and spiritual guidance. I was overwhelmed by the pain, the mental anguish that I had carried from my past. I was miserable and tired from battling with the defeat of worrying about my life ending tragically. My life was under attack by Satan and the demons that he sent to destroy me. There are generational curses in my blood line that tried to take over me. I was a victim to the spirit of rage; I struggled for years with loss of identity, mental anguish, anxiety, poverty, and genetic diseases, etc.

I learned to fight back through prayer. I learned to have patience while enduring the changes that I needed to make. I had to stop doing things that opened the doors of deception. When I approached matters spiritually by reading more about what is spiritual warfare, that is when the light bulb came on. There was a reason why Satan was after me. I didn't understand that the Lord was preparing me to be used for His glory. There is an assignment that God planned for my life. The way things were happening, I was compelled to get closer to finding God's will for my life.

I needed to stop running toward the destruction and start walking with the Lord. I slowly learned to listen to God by reading the Holy Bible on a daily basis. God began to reveal His Spirit to me. I knew that a change was happening in my life. He took me through a process of purging my mind, heart, soul, and spirit. I was messed up with my negative thinking and harboring feelings of anger. The pain was buried deep inside crevices of my soul. I cried many days and nights while pleading my cause to the Lord for mercy. It was severe and very painful; I thought the process was never going to end, because several seasons had come and gone.

After the purging process, I was able to gain strength as I moved forward. The new battles that I had to face opened my spiritual eyes to discern how to combat situations. I was able to recognize head-on the signs and the attacks that were coming at me. The Lord quickened my spirit to pray and to use godly wisdom as I faced the mountains in my life. I no longer wavered in my flesh or sought after carnal advice to counsel me through most matters. There was a difference in how I thought about things; God renewed my mind by sharpening my memory to apply His word to my situations. The Holy Spirit was working in my life by revealing things before they happened, so that I would know how to fight and become victorious.

I was amazed by how the Lord was moving in my life. I would sit and cry about it, because I was winning this time. I rejoiced because He was with me going through the battles that I encountered. I could see that everything was aligning up on my path. The most incredible part was realizing that God was revealing His words to me through my dreams. I was intrigued by all of this and compelled to follow His Spirit by writing down the dreams and the melodies of words He was birthing in me.

I honor God with my heart and life, because He thought more of me than I did of myself and valued me enough to love me this way. I praise Him, and the glory belongs to Him alone. I desire to be available at all times to do

God's will. I owe Him something, so I decided to start by saying thank You and sharing my testimony. It is apparent that God's love and a touch from Him is all I need.

The joy that I have is overwhelming, because I can feel God's Spirit is with me when I'm ministering to others about Him. There is a price to be used by the Lord, and everything that I had to endure prepared me. I am humble to serve in any capacity. The reward is eternal life, and that's the prize for which I'm laboring. It doesn't matter to me where He puts me as long as I don't quit the race.

My heart is in this because I know how deep I was in darkness. My experience in getting to know Him for myself has been an uphill climb. Now I feel like I am truly loved, because God is shining His glory on me. I would have never fathomed that things for me were going to be like this. I dare not put God in a box, because He is wonderful, sweet, and merciful to those who cry out to Him. The good that's inside of me is all because He put it there. I'm no longer wasting my life away. I know God in an intimate way and He forgave me for all the sins I committed. I understand His grace; no one can change or stop the way God's grace and salvation was given as a gift to mankind, Jesus paid for it all at the cross with His blood. I serve a God of second chances; I'm glad that I got to know Him.

I'm striving toward receiving my crown, and that requires determination. Wherever the Lord sends me, I am ready to give Him praise. The direction my life is heading feels completely divine. The blessings that are on my life have caused me to stay before the Lord with a contrite heart and to live in obedience to God's commands. When God moves in your life, the only thing to do is to obey Him. The things that are seen with our physical eyes were unseen before being manifest. The Lord gives mankind the ability to see and proclaim the things that are invisible before they are seen in the natural. He has full control over our body, spirit, and dreams.

As you hold this book , it is the manifestation of where God can take you if you obey and believe that He lives. When you see the dream that God has for you, write the vision, and make it plain (Habakkuk. 2:3). Many blessings are raining from the throne; now start proclaiming your dream.

Generational Prayers

Lord, I pray for understanding
When my life seems hard
I cannot figure things out
My soul is crying out to You
I'm empty inside and need Your love
Let me know that You hear my prayers
I cannot see Your face
But I'm praying from my heart
I know of no other God
Upon this journey called life
I was born to call on You
By faith it was planted within
From generation to generation
You are Lord of lords and King of kings
Thank You for being my inheritance

Labors of Love

When life gets hard, I will be there
You are not a mistake
My love is all that you need
When in doubt cry out to Me
I will send you rain to replenish your hope
There's nothing too hard for Me
I move things in orbit to rotate the earth
Believe I AM I AM the great I AM
The earth is Mine and you are too
I'll always love you even if you don't believe
Remember to pray
I am listening
My labors of love are sent from above

Indescribable

To behold such reverence
As You breathe life into my being
Mere words are not enough
My mind cannot fathom more
Like an endless waterfall
No one can contain who You are
While seasons bloom and bear fruit
Sounds of chirping are within the air
As heaven shines Your light upon the ocean
To capture an awe of glory
Radiates the praise that belongs to You
As the wind blows softly upon the living
Beautiful and glorious are Yours forever
A God that loves and forgives all wrongs
While Your Spirit resides in heaven and earth
Presently there are not enough words to reveal
Your infinite power, grace, and mercy
To God be the glory

Obedience

God, Your will is perfect
I pray to keep Your word
Draw closer to my heart
Please give me a mind of peace
When I am faced with dilemmas
I will trust Your power to keep me
I have made many mistakes
I never want to take it for granted
Therefore I am pleading for Your help
Please guide me and protect my lips
My heart seeks
Lord, I want what You want

Denise P. Ford

Butterfly Stretch

I'm feeling down as the days go by
Lord, are You purging me?
I cannot seem to stop crying
On the outside of my life things appear fine
My soul feels stretched from within
Please be gentle with me
During the nights I cry in despair
I'm praying for You to be there
To help me rise out of this cocoon
All of my hope is in Your hands
When it's time to emerge
I pray to soar high like a butterfly

Beautiful Distractions

While the melodies sing
My heart is full of joy
On a warm summer's day
As the sun rises
Dew drops are falling
While tulips and roses bloom
My spirit sings along
There are sounds of echoes
To and fro within the universe
Joy, oh joy, another day
My thoughts are pleasant
As bliss fills the air
A colorful world that surrounds me
How captivating and awe-inspiring
As I witness God's beauty

About the Author

Denise P. Ford is a native of Detroit, Michigan. Since her life was transitioned to a spiritual calling, she has started on the path that God has predestined for her in ministry. She is currently pursuing the call to inspire hope to people from all walks of life.

She has a love for inspiration and poetry. Her journey is to advocate for women and children, victims of domestic abuse and violence. She has witnessed that mountains are movable; her faith is sown on the foundation of God's plans for her life. While she works toward the vision of establishing an outreach ministry, her words of inspiration are a testimony of how good God's grace truly is.

Denise and her husband, Thomas, are the parents of six children and four grandchildren. They have committed to following the call on their lives to help make a positive impact on the lives of others. Through their journeys and aspirations, a legacy of faith and hope will be established.

www.ingramcontent.com/pod-product-compliance
Lightning Source LLC
Chambersburg PA
CBHW051042030426
42339CB00006B/161